Keeping Your Indoor Cat Happy and Healthy

Arden Moore

CONTENTS

Introduction

My first cat, Corky, was an adventurous Siamese who came to my whistle, swam with my family's two dogs, and brought me a few birds as birthday presents. I was 12 and living in a rural Indiana neighborhood with a lake in the backyard. As soon as I stepped off the school bus each afternoon, I'd let out a loud whistle and Corky would come running down the street to greet me. In the middle of the night, when Corky finished prowling and wanted to come inside, he would meow outside my bedroom window. I would lift up the screen and watch him hop inside and find a comfy spot at the foot of my bed.

Cats and dogs ran free all over the neighborhood without ID tags and rarely with collars. All of us knew all the dogs and cats by name. And we knew who owned them. We never worried about them getting hit by cars, getting lost, or harming anyone.

Times have changed. It's rare that we know all the neighbors in our block, let alone their pets' name. Many of us live in apartments, townhouses, or homes with little or no yards. With fast-moving cars, stray dogs, fleas and ticks, and people who abuse animals, the great outdoors isn't so safe anymore for free-roaming cats.

The safest and best place for cats these days is right inside your home. As much as I loved the freedom that Corky had 30 years ago, I'm glad that my latest bunch — Little Guy, Callie, and Murphy — live safely inside my southern California home. The truth is, they run the place. It's become a cat castle.

Some 72 million American households include cats. Of them, nearly 80 percent of owners brag about their beloved cats, according to the latest survey by the American Pet Products Manufacturers Association. And 79 percent fess up that they allow their cats to sleep on their beds at night, and 27 percent celebrate their cats' birthday.

Why Indoors Is Best

Roaming cats face an increased risk of injury and exposure to infectious diseases. Indoor cats live longer than their outdoor counterparts. Statistics from the Humane Society of the United States indicate that the cat who makes his home outside lives to be five, on average. Cats kept inside can live into their early 20s.

Let's admit it: We adore these felines. And we want to keep them healthy and happy for a long, long time. In this booklet, I'll show you how to turn your house into a cat haven, a place of fun, security, and contentment. Read on!

Cat Chat

When was the last time you had a conversation with your cat? No, I'm not talking about those one-sided conversations like, "Come here, Toby, it's time for your medicine" or "Bikini, get down from the top of the TV." Two-way communication is important to maintain between you and your cat. These social creatures deserve — and occasionally demand — your attention. The happiest housebound cats are those who feel like part of the family. So speak with your cat often. Greet her when you come home. Acknowledge her when you stride past her on the way to the kitchen. Let her know that she matters in your life.

Speak in soothing, flattering tones so she won't feel neglected. And always use your cat's name each time you begin a conversation with her. It helps her recognize her name and, more importantly, she learns to associate hearing you speak her name with good experiences such as receiving praise, getting a friendly head scratch, or being offered tasty treats.

As silly as it may sound, try mimicking your cat's sounds once in awhile. When your cat meows at you, she may be asking, "Hey, did you see that bird perched on the power line across the street?" Give her a half-wink look and meow back. Don't worry if your meow translates into "Yes, it *is* a sunny day." Words can get lost in the translation, but not your good intentions. Your cat will appreciate even your most feeble attempts at Cat Speak.

Cats don't need to speak English. Their simple language suits them just fine, thank you. But if you pay close attention, you'll discover that cats communicate clearly through different vocal sounds and body language. Unlike us, cats don't clutter their vocabularies with slang, double meanings, or sarcasm.

Don't forget how a cat communicates the most: through her body language. If she rubs against your leg — and you know she will — she is marking you. It's her friendly way of telling other scent-skilled animals, "Hey, this is *mine*." Don't worry. It's a form of feline flattery.

Pay attention to her tail. She uses it as mood barometer. When it is held loosely upright during a walk, she is signaling confidence and contentment. When she flicks the tip of her tail at you, she is conveying, "Hello, my good pal." A light twitching motion means relaxed alertness. On the other hand, when the tail puffs out like a pipe cleaner, she feels spooked and frightened. And when the tail whips side to side or thumps repeatedly on the floor, she is definitely irked and angered by something or someone.

Whether speaking or using body cues, cats always communicate directly and never play mind games. As novelist Lewis Carroll wrote, "You might not like what they have to say, but cats will never deceive you."

They are certainly not shy in expressing what they want. When the sun pokes up above the horizon each morning, my cats line up at the foot of my bed and begin full-throttled purrs followed by a three-part harmony of me-OWS (accent is on the second syllable). The minute I open an eye, Callie, the ringleader, nudges my pillow up with her head. It's their direct way of reminding me that it's time for their spoonfuls of wet cat food (a once-a-day event). Obediently, I stumble into the kitchen and prepare their breakfasts. This ritual occurs every morning, rain or shine. They've communicated — and trained me — well.

A cat with its tail held high and head up is happy, confident, and glad to see you.

What Did You Say?

Here are a few translations of your cat's communication:

Meow. Your cat delivers this sound when she demands your attention. She may be saying, "Come see me play — now!" or "It's late. Where have you been all night?"

Chirp. This musical trilling sound ends in a question mark. It conveys a friendly greeting given only to people, not other cats. It can mean "Welcome home" or "I just woke up from my nap and it's really good to see you."

Purr. Cats have the unique skill of breathing in and out while making this engine revving sound with their mouths closed. Cats purr when they are happy — like during a massage — and, strangely, when they confront a stressful situation, such as a vet visit.

Hiss. Your cat is plainly telling you to "back off." If the warning is unheeded, a defensive swipe of the paw likely will follow.

Make Your Home a Purr-fect Palace

You can make your home fit for a cat without spending a lot of money, whether you live in a penthouse, a ranch home, a basement apartment, or a townhouse in the city, suburbs, or country. All you have to do is help your cats feel like they belong, like they are viable members of the household. They need their own spaces. You can claim the couch and the recliner; they have dibs on the scratching post and the top shelf of the bookcase.

Cat-pleasing household items to consider include the following:

Scratching post. One is a must. Two or more in different rooms is even better. Cats with claws need a place to hone their nails, mark their territories, and release their predatory aggressiveness. The multitiered ones are more expensive, but they double as "forts" for cats to play on.

Comfy napping accoutrements. Situate big, soft pillows or folded blankets in strategic places around your home. Cats like them on the foot of your bed, near a sunny window, and in the closet. Make sure these sleeping materials are washable and clean them once a month.

Window platforms. Pet shops and many retail stores sell self-supporting platforms that attach to window frames to offer your cats a high perch. The platform is supported by bars with suction cups on their ends. The bars extend down from the platform and then bend in to press against the wall below the window. It's physics and it's sturdy and safe (and no need to drill holes into the drywall). Many platforms feature cozy fleece seats that cats love to snooze on.

Cat condo. Cats love to hide out in comfy cat-size spaces; carpet-covered kitty condos fit the bill. Simple cat condos are no more than glorified "caves." More complex cat condos offer enclosed sleeping spaces as well as a variety of platforms for perching, lounging, hiding, and scratching.

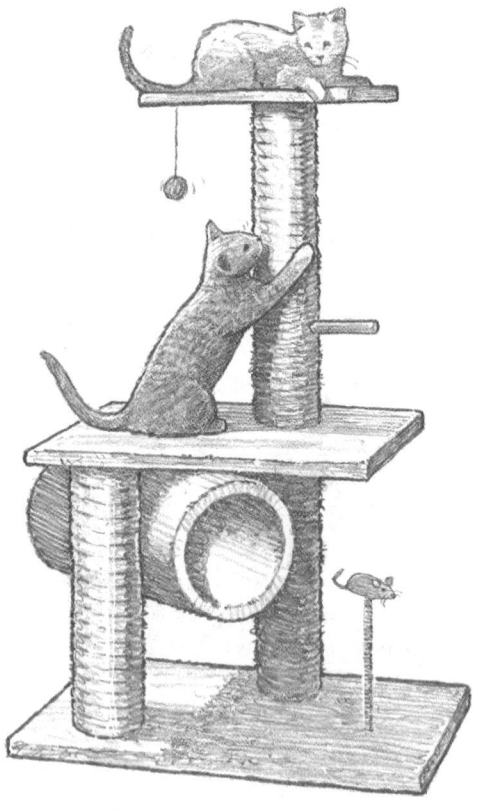

Multitiered cat condos, also known as cat trees, offer many different platforms for napping, hiding, scratching, and otherwise lounging about.

Welcoming Your Cat into Your Daily Routines

Your actions and attitudes also influence how well your cat takes to indoor living. The most important thing is to establish a routine. Cats are creatures of habit. And they quickly learn how to train us to cater to their needs and whims. They wake us up when they want to be served food, rub against our legs when they want some attention or a minimassage, and drop toys at our feet or on the newspaper we're reading when it's time to play. Here are some ways to make your cat feel like she is a full-fledged member of the household:

- After you complete your morning grooming routine, groom your cat. Cats love to be brushed; it not only keeps their coat healthy but also feels great — like having an extended back-scratching session! Your cat will soon learn to sit waiting for you in the bedroom as you get ready for the day.
- Invite your cat to hang around with you and explore your closet while you're deciding what to wear each morning.
- Got a cat who hates shut bathroom doors? When you're planning to pamper yourself with a well-deserved bubble bath, place an old towel or sweatshirt on top of the laundry basket lid or toilet lid as a comfy perch for your nosy cat. Let her sit and enjoy the fragrance of the bubble bath and the moist heat in the air without getting a drop of water on her fur. It's like a cat sauna. Resist the playful temptation to sprinkle water on your cat. Use this opportunity to strengthen your bond of trust.
- Open the window blinds every morning to allow sunshine to pour in and to give your cat a warm perch for observing outdoor activities.
- During cold winters, wrap your cat in warm towels plucked from the dryer to take the chill out of his coat. Prevent static electricity by keeping your house at 50 percent humidity with a couple of humidifiers humming in high-traffic locations.
- Fill your cats' water bowl with fresh water every morning and every evening. Instead of tap water, give them a healthier source — bottled water or filtered water.
- Clean out the litter box each morning. Change it weekly. Cats like clean bathrooms and may go elsewhere if the litter box is dirty and smelly. Sprinkle baking soda into the litter to help reduce its odor.

The Cat's Meow

A friend's home in San Diego is the ultimate cat's meow. Each room outdoes the previous one in terms of feline appeal. There are rugs with smiling cat faces on wooden floors. Toys everywhere. Floor-to-ceiling scratching posts. Cat-sized holes in the upper walls near the ceiling, with brightly colored catwalks cascading and weaving down to the floor. This three-bedroom ranch house belongs to Bob and Francis Walker — at least that's what the deed reads. But in truth, the real rulers of this domain are the nearly dozen cats (the numbers vary) and one dog.

Calafia, Beauregard, Frank-the-Friendly-Kitten, and the rest of the gang regard this almost-bay view home as their lofty feline playhouse. There are high perches for catnapping, hiding places from which to pounce, and more than 100 feet of catwalks. The home even boasts a cats-only clubhouse, a room built into the top of the bedroom closet, with an opening big enough only for felines. Couches are covered with plastic, and absent are flowers in vases just waiting to be knocked over. Window perches are everywhere for afternoon siestas.

My friend Bob tries to explain this cat makeover: "If possession is nine-tenths of the law, then our place is truly the cats house," he says. "They spend more time there than we do. We believe our cats are safer living indoors and need a place that perks their curiosity and makes them feel safe."

Once a year, the Walkers sponsor an open house for curious visitors, most of them cat lovers. The Walkers donate the price of admission to the National Cat Protection Society in the hope that other cat owners will pick up some pointers on how to make their homes more feline-friendly.

Cat-Proofing Your Home

My friend Barbara has four cats sharing her two-bedroom apartment, but you would never know she runs a multicat household. Her place is immaculate and smells like fresh-cut flowers on a spring day. She confirms what I've known for a long time: Cat owners have some of the neatest, cleanest homes. That's because responsible owners have learned long ago how to clear the air, so to speak, so that visitors don't smell a cat before they see one. Cat owners also have learned (probably the hard way) how to keep valuables out of paw's reach.

When it comes down to it, cats don't know the price difference between your antique crystal flower vase and a paper wad. Nor do they really care. It's up to us to cat-proof our homes. So, think like a cat when you decorate. Take a room-by-room inventory and try to second-guess what might entice your curious, adventurous cat.

Recognize that your cat likes high places and will insist on walking on shelves. Realize that food left on the kitchen counter is too much of a temptation for even the best-behaved feline to ignore. Practice the same parenting skills you've used raising toddlers or babysitting grandchildren:

- Place childproof latches on doors housing cat food or no-cats-allowed items.
- Tuck safety cords out of sight.
- Place fragile valuables beyond harm's reach.
- Keep the dryer door shut.
- Don't place stacks of books or magazines where they can easily topple.

Stop Trouble Before It Starts

Got a cat who likes to terrorize the toilet paper roll? Got a sweater eater or coin licker? Follow these hints for keeping your feline friend safe and out of trouble.

- **Secure the toilet paper.** Do you come home and find streamers of tissue paper down the hallway? Curb this behavior by securing the roll with a rubber band. And shift your cat's attention to a more acceptable attraction, like a toy mouse dangling on a cord from a doorknob.
- **Know your cat's hiding places.** Cats are drawn to tiny, cozy, enclosed places. Make sure that your cat isn't harboring inside a dresser drawer, cupboard, closet, or washer/dryer when you close the door. (When first-time visitors come to my home, I always know where to find Little Guy. He ducks into the bottom shelf of my antique dresser given to me by my grandmother. All I see on top of my folded shorts and T-shirts is a pair of nervous, wide green eyes staring back at me.)

- **Keep woolens out of reach.** Stow wool and knit blankets in a trunk or nearby closet when they're not in use. Cats who eat these fabrics and other nonfood objects are suffering from pica syndrome. Eating such items can cause obstruction of the intestinal tract and is potentially toxic.
- **Learn to compromise about snoozing spots.** Drape cotton sheets or throw blankets over recliners and sofas so that your cat can snooze without depositing a mountain of hair on your furniture. Just wash these coverings once a week and you'll save on vacuuming time and dry-cleaning bills.
- **Test the tension of your window screens regularly.** Cats love to lounge on windowsills when the windows are open. Cats can accidentally fall out the window if the screen is not secure and taut.
- **Store coins in jars with lids.** Pennies contain zinc, a metal that is toxic to cats. Also stash sewing needles, thumbtacks, earrings, rubber bands, buttons, and other small items in containers or drawers.
- **Keep a fitted sheet on the underside of your bed.** This will prevent your cat from eating the synthetic materials on the bottom of the box spring.
- **Store bath items out of reach.** Elevate your shampoo, conditioner, soap, and razor in your shower area out of paw's reach. Never leave dental floss dangling in an open wastebasket. Your curious cat could ingest it and possibly choke to death. Deposit used floss into trash cans with lids.
- **Don't let your cat roam inside your garage.** Most types of antifreeze contain ethylene glycol (EG), a sweet temptation that is deadly to cats. It only takes a couple ounces of antifreeze to kill a cat. EG crystallizes and attacks the kidneys.
- **Outwit your counter-climbing feline.** Break your cat of the habit of leaping on the dining room table or kitchen counters with double-sided tape. Cats rely on their feet to mark their territories, so they like to keep their paws impeccably clean. When a cat jumps on a counter and lands on the sticky tape, she hates the sensation and immediately jumps down to search for a friendlier high spot. For kitchen counters, you can also fill a cookie sheet with water as a booby trap. This strategy is especially effective because it works 24 hours a day, even when you're gone. And the best news: Your cat won't connect you with the tape, so you can be blame-free!

Stop Dangerous Chewing

Many cats enjoy chewing electric cords, a habit that is nasty, expensive, and potentially dangerous. You can place conduit devices over the cords to stop the chewing. Or coat the cords with smells cats abhor: hair spray, cayenne pepper spray, or citrus-smelling agents.

That takes care of step 1. Step 2 is to figure out why your cat is chewing. Often, it is a symptom of separation anxiety. Your cat loves and needs you too much. So, don't make a big deal out of your arrivals or departures. Leave behind a piece of your clothing and a tape recording playing your voice to give your cat some comfort while you're not at home.

Avoid Poisonous Houseplants

If you think your cat is safe indoors, think again. Is your home adorned with plants? Many popular indoor plants are downright deadly to cats who munch on their leaves. Plants add a feel of coziness and serenity to any home, but shop smart.

Most cats like nothing better than nibbling on houseplants. You must keep all of your houseplants beyond feline reach.

Steer clear of the following lineup of plants. All of them are poisonous to cats:

- African violet
- American mistletoe
- Azalea
- Buttercup
- Christmas cacti
- Dieffenbachia
- Foxglove
- Horse chestnut
- Hyacinth
- Hydrangea
- Iris
- Lily of the valley
- Morning glory
- Ornamental tobacco
- Philodendron
- Poinsettia
- Poison hemlock
- Poppy
- Rhododendron ficus
- Rubber plant
- Tomato vines
- Tulip

For a complete list of poisonous plants, click on the Humane Society of the United States's Web site at www.hsus.org. In the meantime, if you catch your cat munching on a houseplant, divert her attention by shaking a can of pennies. The loud noise will stop her in midchew. Then bring her to a patch of kitty grass (see the following section); if she starts munching on these alternative greens, praise and pet her.

In an Emergency

Signs of possible poisoning include abdominal pain, vomiting, diarrhea, listlessness, muscle tremors, lack of coordination, and fever. If your cat is experiencing these symptoms and you suspect poisoning, call the National Animal Poison Control Center at (900) 680-0000. You will be billed $45 per case to your phone bill with no time limit. Alternatively, phone (888) 426-4435, which bills the same fee to any major credit card. Professionals staff this hotline 24 hours a day, seven days a week.

Feline-Friendly Indoor Gardening

Love your plants and love your cats? Here's a safe compromise: Hang your plants out of your cat's reach and appease his "green paw" tendencies by providing him with cat-safe plants.

A tray of edible indoor grass tops the list of feline-pleasing greens. Just put some grass seed in soil inside an aluminum pan. Place it in a sunny spot and water it to the point of keeping the soil moist, but not saturated. In no time, grass blades will sprout, and it's a dinner salad for your cat! Potted grass plants satisfy your cat's need to chew and also reduce the incidents of hairballs.

Dill and catnip are also wonderful plants to grow indoors for your cat. Dill is Mother Nature's tummy soother, terrific for curbing indigestion. Catnip is the classic cat herb. A pinch or two of catnip leaves on the scratching post jumpstarts a cat's playful nature.

Catnip has the opposite effect on people — it acts as a relaxant. While your cat acts frisky at night with his catnip, brew yourself a cup of catnip tea. Just put 1 tablespoon of fresh or dried catnip leaves into a cup of boiling water. Let it steep 5 to 10 minutes, strain out the leaves, and sip. By the time you're finished, both you and your cat will be ready for a good night's sleep.

The Inside Scoop on Litter

Does your indoor cat act like a little stinker and go outside the litter box? First, have your veterinarian give your cat a medical exam. If no medical problems are detected, your cat may be sidestepping the litter box because it stinks.

If you religiously clean the box out daily and the behavior persists, try some of these strategies:

- Switch to a new litter and put it in a new, clean box. Some cats develop allergies to certain types of litter. There are lots of types on the market, ranging from the clumping to wheat litters. Avoid litters that are perfumed, especially those with flower or lemon scents. Cats abhor those smells.
- Avoid overfilling the pan. Keep the litter at no more than 2 inches deep.
- Stop using enclosed litter boxes with lids. The urine smell gets trapped inside, inciting some cats to go elsewhere.
- Keep your cat's litter box far from her food and water bowls. Cats instinctively won't eliminate near their food source.

Meow-ve-lous Massage

Step into your cat's paws for a second (figuratively, of course). You're waking up from your third nap of the day and starting to do a yogalike stretch just as your owner bounds your way wearing that silly grin. Now, still imagining yourself as your cat, which of the following would you *purr-fer*?

Scenario 1: "Hey, Callie! Great to see you! Come over here and get some petting!" These shrieking words are followed by a quick series of open-handed thumps pounding on top of your head. Your owner views it as a friendly greeting. You view it as the start of a giant headache.

Scenario 2: "Glad to see you're waking up from your snooze, Callie. Would you like a little kitty massage?" These soothing words are spoken softly. You, as the cat, stand up, stretch, and agree to a 5-minute muscle massage that runs down the spine from your neck to the base of your tail. You feel *meow-ve-lous*.

Indoor cats everywhere have been anxious for me to tell cat owners: Petting is passé. What cats really want are massages. Now, step back into your body and let me show you how to make your cat feel like she's living in a fancy spa resort!

Why Massage?

Regular massages are incredibly good for your indoor cat. This ancient therapeutic treatment does more than pamper. It keeps cats healthy, fit, and feeling fine. Scientists have shown that massage, when done properly, relieves muscle tension and joint stiffness. It also enhances the flow of rich, oxygenated blood throughout the body as well as increases flexibility and range of motion.

And there are more benefits! Regular massage strengthens the cat-owner bond. It's a special time when you can pay attention to and express affection for your cat. I've had a lot of friends tell me their once-aloof cats became interactive members of the household after they started receiving regular massages. Massage builds trust and friendship.

Massage has its medical merits, too. By moving your hands through your cat's coat, you can detect any lumps, cuts, fleas, or ticks. The earlier the detection, the quicker the cure!

Top 10 Tips for the Ultimate Feline Massage

To make massage time enjoyable for both you and your feline friend, here are a few pointers:

1. Let your cat pick the time. Don't try to force a massage just to meet your schedule. Cats can read your body cues and know when you feel stressed or harried.

2. Let your cat pick the place. Among the popular choices are in your arms, on his favorite blanket at the foot of your bed, on a wide windowsill, on a sofa or chair, or even on the carpeted floor.

3. Clean and dry your hands first. All you need are your hands; cats don't need fancy oils, creams, or lotions.

4. Initiate gently. Walk up to your cat slowly and talk to her in a soothing voice. Let her know you want to give her a massage.

5. Stick with using your hands and fingertips. Don't use your fingernails. Don't use your feet, even if you have the most talented toes in your town!

6. Work slowly. Stroke and stretch your cat slowly. This will help your cat relax into the massage and will also help warm the muscles.

7. Hold each limb just below the knee/elbow joint. This allows good flexion — not so much that the cat feels uncomfortable, but enough that he enjoys the stretch.

8. Never press too deeply. Always stroke the muscles in the direction of the heart to improve healthy blood flow. Use an airy touch, light caress, or mild strokes.

9. Detour around an area of recent surgery or an open wound. Gently massage above and below these areas to stimulate blood and nutrient flow to speed healing.

10. Read your cat's body language. You know he loves the massage if he gives you a sleepy half-eyed look, noses you (a cat kiss), or even falls asleep in your hands. You know he would rather be elsewhere when he begins to resist, wiggle, give you a full-pupil glare, and cry, "M-e-o-w!" (the cat equivalent of "Stop!"). End the session and try again when your cat is in a massage mood. My cats seem to prefer massages of just 5 to 10 minutes; any longer and they start to get restless.

Step-by-Step Feline Massage

Step 1: Stretching. If your cat is relaxed, begin the massage by stretching his or her limbs, holding just below the knee/elbow joint. Your cat may object to this if he or she is feeling particularly playful; in that case, skip ahead to step 2.

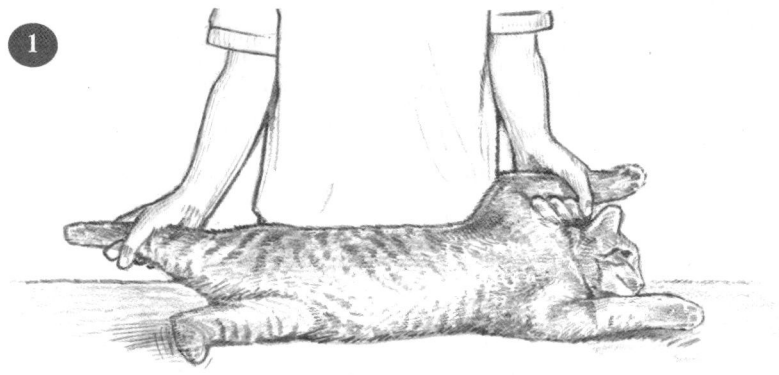

As you're stretching your cat's limbs, hold each limb just below the joint.

Step 2: Effleurage. This basic massage stroke is simply a straight, flowing, continuous motion from head to tail. Steadily slow the pace until the cat is completely relaxed.

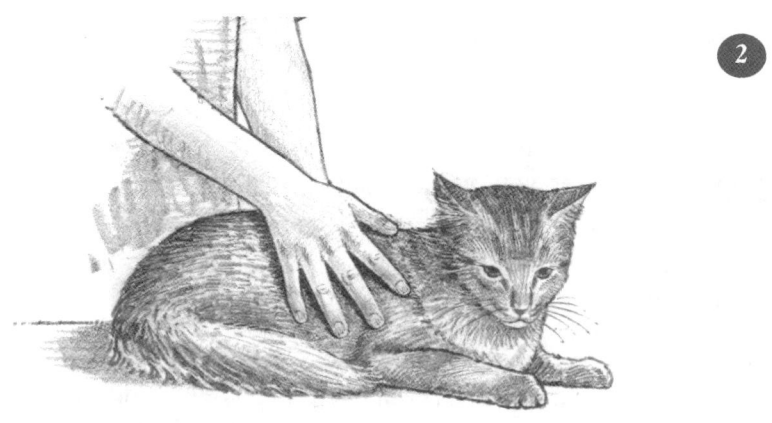

Effleurage, a simple gliding stroke that flows from head to tail, will help your cat relax.

Step 3: Petrissage. Press in a circular motion with the palm of your hand all over the cat's body. "Pick up" handfuls of the soft tissue between your fingers and thumb, then release. Flick your palm and all five fingers in a gentle caressing motion across the spinal area.

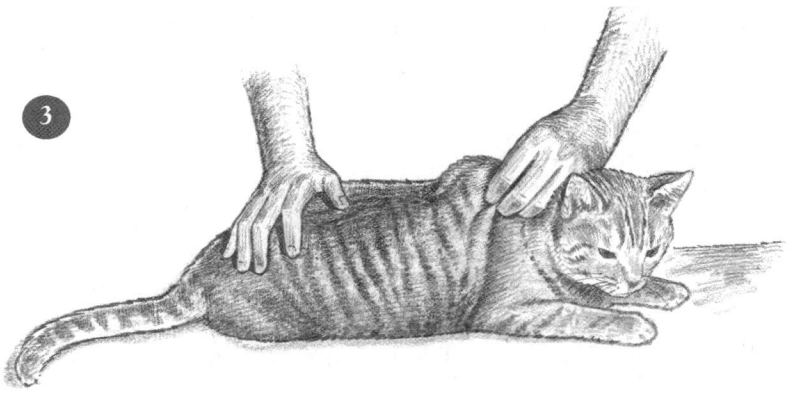

To perform petrissage, a tension-releasing movement, gently pinch up the cat's soft tissue between your fingers and thumb.

Step 4: Wringing and rolling. When your cat is very relaxed, gently push and pull the skin in both hands.

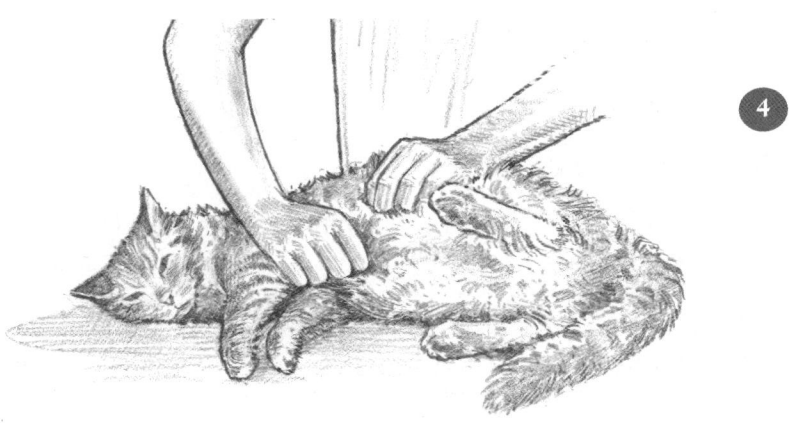

If your cat is enjoying the massage and seems thoroughly relaxed, gently push and pull at the soft tissue with both hands.

Step 5: Stretching. Repeat step 1.

Safety First

Cats are agile and athletic, but they are also curious. The latter trait can put them in harm's way. For that reason, it is best to be prepared for any kitty mishap by keeping a cat first-aid kit handy. I keep mine next to my cats' grooming supplies in the laundry room. Here's a handy checklist of items every feline first-aid kit should include:

- Cotton-tipped swabs for the ears and around the eyes
- Antiseptic wipes
- Cold packs
- Nonstick, sterile gauze pads
- Lightweight adhesive tape that won't stick to wounds
- Antibiotic ointment
- Rectal thermometer
- Hydrocortisone cream
- Diphenhydramine (such as Benadryl) tablets or capsules for stings and bites
- Mineral oil to remove tar and other sticky materials
- Your veterinarian's phone number and emergency hot line

Equally important to keeping a well-stocked kit is learning some basic pet first aid. Contact your local chapter of the Humane Society or the Society for the Prevention of Cruelty to Animals (SPCA) to locate a pet first-aid class in your area. Instructors will teach you how to perform kitty CPR, stop choking episodes, take a temperature, mend a minor wound, and other vital lessons.

Preventive Health Care

You want a startling statistic? Consider this: A pair of mating cats plus their offspring can produce 127,000 cats in only 6 years! Talk about your family tree! Now that would make quite a family reunion!

Because your cat is kept indoors, you may think it's not necessary to have him neutered or her spayed. But in fact, when compared to the unneutered and unspayed feline population:

- On average, spayed and neutered cats live longer, healthier lives.
- Females spayed before their first heat (estrus) cycle are at dramatically less risk for developing urine infections and ovarian and breast cancer.

- Neutered males develop substantially fewer prostrate problems (including cysts, abscesses, and cancer) and have *zero* chance of incurring testicular cancer.
- Altered cats behave better because they are not driven by hormonal urges to escape outside to find a mate.
- Neutered males are less prone to get into catfights.

Every day, about 22,000 homeless cats and dogs are euthanized at animal shelters in the United States. It's vital that you have your cats spayed or neutered. Check with SPAY/USA at (800) 248-SPAY (7729) or Friends of Animals (800) 321-PETS (7387) for low-cost spaying and neutering services in your area. Schedule an appointment during a time that you can spend a couple of days with your cat following surgery to provide comfort and reassurance.

Home-Alone Activities

While you're away from the house, your cats will probably spend their time sleeping. In fact, on average cats spend about 17 hours a day snoozing. However, if you're worried that your cats will be bored or lonely while you're absent, you can keep them occupied with home-alone toys and activities. Not only are these entertaining, but toys help recharge a lethargic cat and tone down the energy level of a frantic youngster. Here is a rundown of some of my cats' favorite playthings:

Cat swat toy. Take an old shoelace from a pair of sneakers. Tie one of your cat's favorite toys on one end and wrap the other end around an interior doorknob so that the toy dangles about 4 or 5 inches off the floor. Most cats can't resist walking by this toy without giving it a good swat.

Nothing to sneeze at. Think of this homemade toy as the Rubik's Cube for cats. Take an empty tissue box and insert a Ping Pong ball inside. Your cat will spend hours trying to fish out this rolling sphere from the narrow opening. It's a real cat teaser, and it gives a second life to a dispensable item.

Kitty treasure hunt. Before you leave for work in the morning, take five or six of your cat's favorite toys — catnip mice, paper wads, shoelaces, whatever — and hide them around your house. Hide a few treats, too. Great hiding spots include under the couch, behind a pillow, and on the windowsill. Play this game with your cat a few times so that she gets the idea. Then, once she is ready to go solo, always praise her for the booty that she finds when you come home. My cats like to dump their found loot next to the scratching post in the living room.

Cat's in the bag. Place a brown paper shopping bag on its side on the floor of your living room or dining room. Be sure to cut off the handles so your cat won't accidentally choke. Just before you head out for work, sprinkle a teaspoon of fresh or dried catnip inside the bag, far in the bag. Your cat's super scenting ability will drive her right into the bag for fun. A sweep of the broom or a quick vacuuming will clean up the mess in seconds.

Cats love to explore any cavelike structure. For hours of home-alone enter-tainment, leave a paper shopping bag on the floor for your cats. Toss a tea-spoon of catnip in the bag before you leave the house.

Cardboard box. Cats like nothing better than to cozy up inside a small area. Stick a medium-sized cardboard box on the floor when you leave. When you get home, don't be surprised if your cat is snoozing inside with some of her favorite toys that she's stowed in with her. My cat Callie lives for cardboard boxes. Separated from her mother at two weeks old and found wandering the streets of Miami, Callie was never weaned. So, she loves to chew on the cardboard box and spit out the pieces, littering the floor. My vet has checked her teeth (tartar-free) and says this is a harmless pastime for a slightly neurotic cat.

Fish aquarium. Cats can spend hours watching fish weave back and forth inside a tank. Make sure that the aquarium's lid is securely attached to avoid any cat pawing episodes. And place the aquarium in a sturdy location to avoid any tipping-over incidents.

Light and sound show. Set your lights and radio on timers so that your cat will hear sounds and see lights coming on and off to make her feel more at ease.

The catnip sock. This is the easiest cat toy ever. Fill an old cotton sock with tissue paper and a pinch of dried catnip leaves. Tie the open end of the sock into a knot. Give it to your cat just before you leave. She'll spend hours batting the sock about the house.

Toys to Avoid

These toys are unsafe for your cats:

- Plastic bags with handles
- Twist-ties for plastic bags; cats love to play with them, but if accidentally swallowed, twist-ties can cause serious damage to a cat's throat and stomach.
- Soft foam balls that shred easily
- Toys with itty-bitty parts or glued-on pieces that can be swallowed
- Empty cellophane cigarette wrappers, which can cause choking
- Coins
- Dental floss

Kitty Tetherball

You can buy one of these clip-on toys or make your own. The lightness of the wire makes the attached fabric ball move erratically, drawing the curiosity of your predator-minded cat. If you opt to make it yourself, just follow these easy steps:

1. Cut a piece of fabric 10 inches square. Fill the center with cotton balls or batting and tie the ends closed with sturdy thread.

2. Cut a 3-foot-long piece of 22-gauge steel wire (available for under $5 at your local hardware store). Attach one end of the wire to the cotton-filled fabric. Use heavy thread to secure its attachment.

3. Attach the other end of the wire through the hole in the handle of a plastic potato-chip-bag clip. Use needle-nose pliers to fasten it snugly so that there are no pointed ends. Connect the clip to a doorjamb or edge of a sturdy piece of furniture.

Interactive Games

Yes, you can teach an old cat — or any cat for that matter — new tricks. You'll enjoy a closer friendship with your cat if you spend 10 minutes a day in one-on-one play. It's good therapy for the both of you. Here are some favorite cat activities that require your participation:

Flashlight tag. At night, shine the flashlight beam against the wall of a darkened room and watch your cat take off in hot purr-suit. Or just dim the lights in a room after dinner. Make sure the area has been cat-proofed so that your feline doesn't knock over anything or run into anything as he chases the light beam.

Hide and seek. With your cat next to you, toss a small treat across the room. As your cat zooms after this tasty prey, slip around the corner out of view and call her name. When she runs to you, reward her with a treat and plenty of praise. Repeat this a few times each day until she gets the idea that it is time to play "find my owner."

Murphy in the middle. My youngest cat, Murphy, loves to play before an audience. When people are around, she will rush to her scratching post in the living room and let out a loud m-e-o-w! as she wrestles a catnip mouse to the ground. That's my cue to solicit a visiting friend to play Murphy's version of a cat-chase-the-mouse game. Murphy sits in the middle of the floor. My friend and I sit about 10 to 12 feet apart on either end. We toss a catnip mouse so that it just barely clears Murphy's ears. That's Murphy's signal to start leaping and snagging the airborne mouse in midflight. Each time she "scores," we lavish her with praise, applaud, and continue this tossing game until Murphy starts grooming herself. That's her way of saying, "Enough fun. It's time to look glamorous."

Follow the feather. Take a peacock feather — or even a long shoelace with a toy mouse tied to the end — and run up and down the hallway. Let the feather or shoelace travel on the floor right past your cat. In no time, she'll be up and joining the chase. Once you have mastered the straight hallway route, you can expand to include the twists and turns of your rooms and stairways. Continually call your cat's name and heap on praise with each catch she makes. It's a great aerobic exercise for the both of you.

The Fine Art of Feline Meditation

Cats have natural know-how when it comes to avoiding stress and staying relaxed. We could learn a lot from our cats. They never lie. They never pretend. What is often mistaken for being aloof or independent is refreshingly mentally positive. Cats walk away from abusive situations and rude people. They go to a quiet, warm, secluded spot. They don't tolerate a stressful situation and let it affect them physically or mentally.

We need to respect our cats' need for solo time. This private time gives them a chance to recharge and renew themselves. Let me illustrate. When you spot your cat sitting by a window or in a favorite sunny spot, it's easy to assume she's just being lazy. But my animal behaviorist friends tell me that cats actually meditate. They tune out the world and exist in the here and now for short periods of time. It's called the art of silence. When they do this, it clears their mind, reduces their heart rate, drops their blood pressure, and brings them a sense of calm.

So, instead of disturbing them, take a lesson from them and give yourself 5 to 10 minutes each day of pure, uninterrupted solitude. Let your cat teach you how to cope with stress.

Bringing the Indoors Out

Indoor cats deserves to smell fresh air and feel warm sunshine on their coats. You can accomplish this without letting your cat roam unchaperoned outside by giving him or her a private room with a view: an outdoor pet enclosure.

Pet enclosures extend the cat-friendly atmosphere of your home into your backyard — safely. Protected inside a sturdy enclosure equipped with scratching posts, ramps, and perches, your cat will get the chance to smell the air, feel the breeze, and get a closer look at birds, squirrels, and other outdoor critters without the perils of being in the wide world on his own. Your cat can even catch bugs!

A cat enclosure allows your cat to visit the great outdoors in safety. They can range from simple 2 x 4 structures with fencing to more elaborate complexes containing cat condos, live trees, and cat-flap doors providing 24-hour access from the house.

Enclosures vary in sizes and shapes. Here are a few tips on helping you get started:

- Check with your city or homeowner's association first to make sure the enclosure won't require a building permit or violate neighborhood construction rules.
- Do a budget to estimate the costs in advance. Include the cost of equipment, materials, and time.
- Take your time building the enclosure or hire someone handy with tools and wood.
- Select quality materials that are sturdy and long lasting. Best choices include plywood; redwood; PVC piping; thick, steel chicken wire; and 4 x 4 blocks of wood. Floor options range from grass and dirt to concrete and carpet. Finally, rely on quality fasteners to prevent accidental openings.
- Be realistic on the size and dimensions. The enclosure should be big enough for your cat to move about easily, but you don't need to match the size of your patio or living room.
- For folks living in apartments, consider patio-style enclosures that fit over double or single windows, giving your cat a private bay window area. Some friends of mine have opted to put their cats in large, collapsible steel crates on their balconies. The crates fold up neatly when not in use.

Regardless of the size or style, make the enclosure comfy for your cats by including bedding materials (thick towels or a cat bed), food, and water. Other options include shelving areas as well as connecting tunnel systems.

Scheduling even 10 minutes a day for your cat to roam and nap inside an enclosure can invigorate her and help chase away any boredom blues. Be close by as she enjoys spending time checking the outdoor world from a safe location.

A final option: If you have an enclosed run in your backyard for your dog, then periodically let your cat use this safe outdoor haven. What should you do with your dog? Use this time to give him a bath with your garden hose. This way you can keep an eye on both your pets.

When Your Cats Are on Their Own

Cats are much more independent than dogs, but if you plan to be away from home more than a couple of days, I recommend that you rely on a trusted neighbor or a professional pet sitter to cater to your cat's needs. Make sure that these cat sitters meet your feline friends in advance. Spell out your cat's likes and dislikes, your house rules, feeding portions, and any of your cat's idiosyncrasies (like hiding under your bedspread or chewing on cardboard boxes).

On your refrigerator door, post info that provides the name of your cat (and nickname); how much, what, and when she eats; the location of the food; instructions for medications; how to contact you and how to reach your veterinarian. You might also introduce your pet sitter to a few of your close neighbors so that they won't be suspicious when the sitter enters your home. In preparing your cat-care list for your pet sitter, make sure the words "Clean litter box daily" rank high. Finally, include nonpet requests, like pick up the newspapers and mail and water the plants.

If you're new to town or don't know how to reach a professional, licensed pet sitter, contact the National Association of Professional Pet Sitters (800-296-PETS or www.petsitters.org) or Pet Sitters International (800-268-SITS or www.petsit.com).

Comfort Zone

When you have to be away from your cat, stick one of your dirty T-shirts at the foot of your bed to help her sleep. Your scent will make her feel secure.

Paws-i-tive ID: Collars, Tags, Tattoos, or Microchips?

Even though you pride yourself on keeping your cat indoors, you still need to practice some precautions in the event your cat suddenly finds herself outside. Try as you may, you can't always prepare for that back door left partially opened by a visiting friend, a loose window screen, or your cat wiggling out of your arms as you step out of your car from a veterinary visit.

It gives you the most sinking feeling to know that your pampered indoor cat is alone, frightened, confused, and hungry somewhere outdoors. According to recent statistics compiled by the Humane Society of the United States, only two of every one hundred cats plucked from the streets who end up in shelters are safely returned to their owners. The prime reason: Most cats found in the streets are not wearing tags.

That's why it is important to keep a collar with identification tags on your cat at all times (except for grooming and bath time). Make sure that the collar fits snugly, that it's neither too tight nor too loose. If you can easily slide just one or two of your fingers under the collar, that's a good fit. Remember that your cat keeps growing, so periodically check the collar's fit. You may need to go up a size.

Getting an ID tag these days is as easy as buying cat food. That's because many pet supermarket stores offer do-it-yourself ID tag-making machines that are easy to operate, inexpensive, and quick. In a few minutes, you can put the pertinent information on a tag of the color, size, and shape of your choice. Veterinary clinics and pet mail-order catalogs also offer a variety of ID tags.

Now, if you own a cat who stubbornly refuses to wear a collar and tag, or you want added insurance, a smart option is to make an appointment with your vet to get a tattoo for your cat's ear. Your cat should be at least 6 months old before getting a tattoo. This unique alpha-numeric code is etched inside your cat's ear where hair won't obscure its presence. All tattoo codes are recorded at a toll-free registry. For more details, visit the Web site: www.tattoo-a-pet.com.

You can also ask your veterinarian to surgically implant a microchip under your cat's skin. About the size of a grain of rice, the microchip is usually implanted between the shoulder blades. Don't worry — it doesn't go so deep as to enter the muscle, and it is made of a material that won't irritate even the most sensitive cats. Many animal shelters — in growing numbers — are equipped with special detection wands so that they can check for identification of rescued cats not wearing collars and tags.

On the Move Again

Over the past five years, my cats have moved with me five times. We've lived in Florida, Pennsylvania, and California in accommodations ranging from sprawling waterfront properties to temporary, tiny apartments with windows facing only one direction. Yet each time, within a day or so, my cats are playing and purring in the new place, proclaiming it as their new domain.

What's my secret? Step up your communication with your cat before, during, and after the move. Strange as it may sound, I talk to my cats a few weeks before the move and let them know what will happen. Yes, strange, beefy men will be coming in and out of the house carting away furniture and belongings. I try to convey a sense of excitement and adventure. And, taking a lesson from the many realtors I've hired, I speak of the perks of the new place. There will be plenty of windowsills where you can perch and bird watch. Yes, this one does have a set of stairs for your nightly workouts, and yes, it does come with an enclosed screened porch.

Holistic Helpers

In the days preceding the move I treat my cats to extra massages (see pages 16–17 for instructions) to help them relax. At the suggestion of some holistic veterinarians, I also add a few drops of Rescue Remedy to my cats' water bowl, starting about 2 weeks before the Big Move. This homeopathic medicine contains a collection of flower essences that naturally help your cat fight stress and feel calm. (It's inexpensive and available at most health food stores and even most drug stores). At the same time, I add a few drops to my glass of water, because cats are savvy about reading our emotions. When you feel calm, it helps them to feel calm. Try it! You both may benefit.

Moving Day

Before you move your cat, run a slightly damp towel across your cat's back. Bring the towel with you to your new place and rub it on the walls, floors, and furniture there. Your cat will recognize his own scent and feel more at ease in the new surroundings.

On moving day, keep your cats inside an empty room (a large bathroom or spare bedroom, depending on the locale). Stock the room with these items:

- A portable radio set on a pop rock station to help drown out the sounds of moving
- A few favorite cat toys, like catnip mice, shoelaces, and a paper wad
- The cats' scratching post
- Food and water bowls with a few treats
- A couple of T-shirts that you have worn at least once but not yet washed
- The litter box
- Pet carriers tucked in the corner, with their doors propped open (secure the door in the open position so that a curious cat won't accidentally shut the door and become trapped inside)

The cats should be the last to be packed and the first to be unloaded once you reach your destination. Before the first box is unloaded off the moving van, place the cats and all the accoutrements you had supplied them with in the old home inside an empty room in the new home. By providing familiar sights, sounds, and smells in a new place, you help your cats adjust to it faster. Wait a few hours after the final boxes are unpacked before letting your cats explore the other parts of the home, one room at a time. Start with rooms with doors you can close and let the cats explore at their own pace. When they seem comfortable in one room, move them on to the next one. This step-by-step introduction builds their confidence and contentment.

Update ID Tags

Add this to your moving checklist: Update your cat's ID tags *before* your move. On the day you get your new telephone number at your new locale, buy your cat a new ID tag. Add it to her collar and remove the old tag *after* you've reached your new locale. If your cat happens to scoot out in the midst of the move, people who find her will have a way to reach you. Hmm . . . if only cats had pagers, we would worry less!

Get Your Cat a Pet Pal

Some cats are so social that they need constant companionship. Getting them a furry playmate can ease their boredom and anxiety while you're away from home.

Making the proper introduction, however, is vital. Ideally, the best furry friendships are between the same species — cat-to-cat — but you can also make winning matches between a cat and a dog, guinea pig, rabbit, bird, and other critters. Aim for complementary personalities whenever feasible. If your cat is an extrovert and bold, pair her up with a cat that is easygoing and willing to play follow the leader.

Murphy is the newest arrival in my home and quickly became buddies with Little Guy and Callie because I heeded these instructions from some of my animal behaviorist friends:

1. Buy your cat a new scratching post a few days ahead of the new pet's arrival. Okay, so it's a bribe, but your cat will associate this prize with an impending positive change.

2. Be patient. Friendships, like Rome, aren't always built in a day. Some cats take weeks, even months, to become paw pals.

3. Plan ahead. Select a large bathroom or spare room to house the new arrival. Place cat necessities in that room: food and water bowls, bedding, litter box, and toys and shut the door so your house cat won't snoop around.

4. Bring the new pet in as quietly and incognito as possible. Try not to let your cat see you entering the door with this animal to avoid any resentment. Don't pussyfoot around. Walk straight to the new cat room and place her inside and shut the door.

5. By now, your house cat will suspect something is different and will be drawn to the door. Let both animals meet each other by sniffing one another from under the door. This helps them get to know one another on their own terms.

6. After a day or so, take a slightly damp towel and rub it on your new animal's back. Then rub this towel on your house cat's back. Take a second damp towel and rub it first on your house cat's back and then on the new arrival's back. Let their scents intermingle.

7. Spend quality one-on-one time with each pet. Pamper them with plenty of praise, hugs, and treats. Make each one feel special.

8. After a few days, switch places. Put your house cat in the spare room for a couple of hours and let the new arrival check out the rest of the house. This helps prevent any possible turf tussles.

9. You're finally ready for the face-to-face introduction. Let your house cat be free to approach the new arrival that you place inside a carrier or on a leash. Let them have plenty of time to approach and sniff. Expect a few hisses — it's your house cat's way of declaring, "Hey, I'm the boss around here."

10. Gradually increase the exposure time of the animals to each other. Give them both food treats, always offering a treat to your house cat first.

Once you feel confident that the two animals can get along, then you can leave them alone unsupervised. Toleration will lead to a playful friendship.

With the proper introductions and plenty of patience, you can provide your cat with well-mannered, friendly companions to share the home with.

Other Storey Books You May Enjoy

50 Simple Ways to Pamper Your Cat, by Arden Moore. In a fun, easy-to-read format, Moore delivers creative, simple, natural, and fun ideas for pampering your cat. From recipes for gourmet treats to grooming hints, herbal flea repellents, pet comfort corners, cat massage techniques, and ways to understand how a cat thinks, this book presents easy-to-implement tips that support a happy, healthy cat and a strong human-feline bond. Paperback. 144 pages. ISBN 1-58017-311-X.

Cat Love: Understanding the Needs and Nature of Your Cat, by Pam Johnson. This essential cat-care guide includes chapters on choosing a cat, nutrition, training and behavior, grooming, and medical and reproduction issues. Voted "Best Cat Book" by the readers of *Cat Fancy* magazine. Paperback. 256 pages. ISBN 0-88266-594-4.

Dr. Kidd's Guide to Herbal Cat Care, by Randy Kidd, D.V.M. Dr. Kidd, a holistic veterinarian and herbalist, explains how herbs can be used as a practical, safe, and effective part of pet care. He explains how herbs work, dosage and potency, and methods for giving herbal remedies to cats. Readers will learn preventive care, approaches to age-related problems, and the treatment of chronic conditions, from calming a nervous cat to getting rid of fleas, treating urinary tract conditions, and strengthening the teeth. Paperback. 192 pages. ISBN 1-58017-188-5.

The Family Butterfly Book, by Rick Mikula. Author Rick Mikula, the "grandfather of butterfly farming," shares his vast knowledge, contagious enthusiasm, and deep respect for these fascinating creatures. Readers will learn how to attract, safely catch, handle, and support butterflies as well as how to create a butterfly habitat and the basics of butterfly farming. The book also features close-ups, including photographs and illustrations of eggs, caterpillars, chrysalises, and butterflies, of 40 favorite North American species. Adults and children alike will enjoy this exciting, intriguing, and environmentally important book. Paperback. Full color. 176 pages. ISBN 1-58017-292-X.

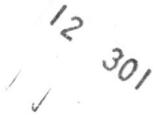